In the morning

BEN	This is the story of one day at the office. It is nine o'clock and people are arriving at work. Jeff is the doorman. Here come Mr. and Mrs. Meyer. They are the bosses. Mr. Meyer likes talking. Mrs. Meyer likes working!
JEFF	(*with a big smile*) Good morning, Mr. Meyer. Good morning, Mrs. Meyer.
MR. AND MRS. MEYER	Good morning, Jeff.
MR. MEYER	(*with a smile*) It's a big day today, Jeff.
JEFF	(*surprised*) Is it?
MRS. MEYER	Mr. Meyer! (*quietly to Jeff*) We can't talk about it. It's a surprise. Do you understand?
JEFF	(*quietly*) OK, Mrs. Meyer. But who is the surprise for and what's it going …
MRS. MEYER	(*quickly*) We want happy workers here. Am I right, Mr. Meyer?
MR. MEYER	Yes, Gladys, we do … Sorry, I mean, yes, *Mrs. Meyer,* we do. We want happy people, with big smiles, on the team!
MRS. MEYER	Have a nice day, Jeff.
MR. MEYER	(*quietly*) And remember, Jeff, don't talk to people about "the big day." Do you understand?
JEFF	I understand. Have a nice day, Mr. and Mrs Meyer.

MR. MEYER   Remember: happy people, Jeff.

MRS. MEYER   Mr. Meyer! *We're* going into our office now!

MR. MEYER   I'm coming, Gladys … I mean, *Mrs. Meyer.*

(*They go into their office and Jim arrives.*)

It is nine o'clock and people are arriving at work.

2

JIM	(*with a smile*) Good morning, Jeff.
JEFF	Hi, Jim. It's the big day today!
JIM	(*puzzled*) Is it?
JEFF	Yes, it is. *You* know that!
JIM	(*very puzzled*) Oh, yes … of course I do. It *is* a very *important* day today. I remember now.
JEFF	Have a nice day, Jim.
JIM	(*unhappily*) You have a nice day, too, Jeff.
	(*Jim goes quickly into a big office. It is behind Mr. and Mrs. Meyer's office. Mia arrives.*)
MIA	(*with a big smile*) Hi, Jeff.
JEFF	Hi, Mia. It's going to be an important day today.
MIA	(*puzzled*) Is it?
JEFF:	Yes, it is. You know that.
MIA:	Oh, yes … of course I know that. Is it going to be another *difficult* day?
JEFF	(*with a smile*) You have a nice day, Mia!
MIA	(*unhappily*) You, too, Jeff. (*She goes into the big office.*)
	(*Liz, Alvin, and Kurt arrive. They are talking happily.*)
LIZ, ALVIN, KURT	Hi, Jeff.
JEFF	Hi. It's going to be a difficult day.
LIZ:	Why is it going to be a difficult day?

3

JEFF	(*with a smile*) I can't answer that question!
ALVIN	What are you talking about, Jeff?
KURT	Jeff, we don't understand. What do you mean?
	(*Ann arrives. Liz, Alvin, Kurt, and Jeff are unhappy.*)
ANN	(*to Liz, Kurt, Alvin, and Jeff*) Hi. What's wrong?
LIZ, KURT, ALVIN, JEFF	(*unhappily*) Hi, Ann.
LIZ	(*to Ann*) It's going to be a long day today!
ANN	Oh, no, not another bad day. Let's go. It's late. Have a nice day, Jeff.
JEFF	Goodbye. Have a happy day!
	(*Liz, Kurt, Alvin, and Ann go slowly and unhappily into the big office. Dylan arrives.*)
DYLAN	(*with a smile*) Hi, Jeff. Am I late?
JEFF	No, you're never late—but Sadie is often late.
DYLAN	Sadie is not *often* late. She's *sometimes* late in the morning because she works late in the evening!
JEFF	It's going to be a *bad* day, you know!
DYLAN	Why is it going to be a bad day?
JEFF	It's going to be a long and bad day! Or was it a *big* day? Did Mr. Meyer say "a bad surprise" or "a good surprise?"
DYLAN	(*puzzled and unhappy*) I can't talk now, Jeff! Have a nice day.

4

(*Dylan goes quickly into the big office. Sadie arrives.*)

JEFF	Hi, Sadie. You're late again!
SADIE	I am a little late, Jeff, but I worked very late yesterday. I arrived home at eleven o'clock.
JEFF	That was late! Are you a slow worker?
SADIE	(*with a smile*) No, Jeff, but we have a lot of work.
JEFF	(*quietly to Sadie*) Mrs. Meyer talked about a "surprise" today.
SADIE	Oh? What did she say?

"Hi, Sadie. You're late again!"

5

JEFF	I'm sorry, Sadie. I can't talk about it. But I can say this: it is *not* going to be a good day! (*happily*) Have a nice day, Sadie.
SADIE	(*unhappily*) See you later, Jeff. (*She goes into the big office.*)
	(*Jeff calls Mrs. Meyer on the telephone. He talks very quietly.*)
JEFF	Hello. Mrs. Meyer, is that you? ... Jeff here. ... I'm calling because Sadie was late today *again*. ... Yes, Mrs. Meyer. Thank you. Goodbye.

"Hello. Mrs. Meyer, is that you?"

In the office

BEN	The office workers are puzzled and unhappy. Now Sadie comes in. She is the team leader. Everybody likes her. She is a good boss.
SADIE	Hi!
THE OFFICE WORKERS	Hi, Sadie.
LIZ	(*to Sadie*) Nice dress!
SADIE	Thanks. It's new.
MIA	I like the color.
KURT	Me, too.
ANN	Was it expensive?
SADIE	Yes, very.
KURT	(*to Sadie*) Can I ask you a question about today?
SADIE	Yes, of course. What do you want to know?
KURT	Is there an important team meeting today?
SADIE	(*puzzled*) No, there isn't. (*She goes and sits down.*)
DYLAN	(*to the team*) I don't understand. Why is it a big day?
MIA	Is there going to be a meeting about pay?
JIM	I'd like a raise.
EVERYBODY	Me, too.

ANN	Is there going to be a meeting about vacations? I need a vacation—soon!
EVERYBODY	Me, too!
ALVIN	Maybe a famous person is coming.
ANN	Who?
MIA	(*talking on the telephone*) Mr. and Mrs. Meyer's office ... Yes, of course ... Who is calling please? (*She writes the name of the caller and then she calls Mr. Meyer.*) ... Mr. Meyer? I have a Mr. Joe Ellis on the phone for you.
ANN	Is *he* famous?
LIZ	No, he isn't!
JIM	I don't understand. Jeff said "a big day"!
MIA	Let's think. What can it be? ... An important day!
KURT, ALVIN, LIZ	A difficult day!
ANN	A long day!
DYLAN	A bad day!
SADIE	Jeff said, "a surprise." What did he mean?
ALVIN	A good surprise or a bad surprise?
ANN	Let's ask the bosses.
LIZ	We can't.
ANN	Why not?
MIA	Because maybe they talked to us about it. Maybe

it's *very* important and we don't remember it!

DYLAN   What can we do?

SADIE   Let's work now. We can talk later. We have a lot of work.

EVERYBODY   (*unhappily*) OK. You're right.

"Let's think. What can it be?"

In the cafeteria

BEN   We are now in the cafeteria. There is a long line of people. Mr. and Mrs. Meyer are at the front of the line. Alvin is standing behind them—then Liz, Dylan, Jim, Ann, Mia, Kurt, and Jeff. Sadie is at the back.

SADIE	(*to Jeff and Kurt*) Look! Mr. and Mrs. Meyer are at the front of the line. What are they talking about?
KURT	(*to Ann and Mia*) Can Dylan and Jim hear the bosses?
ANN	(*to Dylan and Jim*) Are Liz and Alvin listening to Mr. and Mrs. Meyer?
DYLAN	(*to Alvin and Liz, quietly*) What are the bosses saying? Can you hear?
ALVIN	(*quietly*) Quiet! I'm going to listen.
MRS. MEYER	(*to Mr. Meyer*) Maybe we can meet with them late this afternoon? We can talk about my idea.
ALVIN	(*quietly to Liz, puzzled*) Did they say, "Maybe meet Maria at eight, after June?"
LIZ	(*quietly to Dylan, puzzled*) Maybe they said, "Sadie and Mia wait in the street in June."
JIM	(*quietly to Dylan*) What did they say?

"What did they say?

10

DYLAN	(*quietly to Jim, puzzled*) "Sadie in Korea with Kate on her feet soon!"
JIM	(*to Ann*) Sadie in Korea, or was it on the moon?
MIA	(*to Ann*) Sadie's going to the moon? What do they mean?
ANN	(*to Mia*) I don't know! I think they mean, "Sadie is going to the moon soon."
MIA	(*to Kurt*) Sadie's *going*?
KURT	(*to Jeff*) No! Is Sadie going? We need her.
JEFF	(*to Sadie*) They're talking about you!
SADIE	(*to Jeff*) Why? I don't understand.
JEFF	(*to Kurt*) She doesn't understand.
KURT	(*to Mia*) *They* don't want to stand.
MIA	(*to Ann*) Say, "give me your hand."
ANN	(*to Jim*) Give me your hand!
JIM	(*puzzled, to Dylan*) Ann wants my hand.
DYLAN	(*to Liz*) Ann wants Jim's hand!
LIZ	(*to Dylan*) No, she doesn't. You didn't understand! Quiet! (*quietly to Alvin*) What are they saying now?
MR. MEYER	Maybe Joe can come, too?
MRS. MEYER	Let's talk about my plan.
ALVIN	(*quickly back to Liz*) They said "Joe," "blue," "maybe," and "talk in Iran."
LIZ	(*to Dylan*) Joe and you walked out with Ann?

11

DYLAN	(*quickly to Jim and Ann*) I think they said, "Sadie and Joe are going to Sudan."
ANN	(*to Mia*) Sadie and Joe are going to Sudan!
MIA	(*quickly to Kurt*) Maybe she and Joe are going to go.
KURT	(*to Mia*) Go where?
JEFF	No! I know. Sadie is going! (*to Sadie*) They don't want you here. You arrive late, and you're slow. They want Joe. That's the surprise.
SADIE	(*to Jeff, Kurt, and Mia*) Oh, no! Who is Joe? What does this mean?
KURT	He's new.
SADIE	What am I going to do?
MIA	But you're a good team leader. We don't want Joe. Sadie, don't go!

Later that afternoon

BEN	The bosses are coming into the big office with Jeff. They are smiling.
MRS. MEYER	Good afternoon, team! We would like a quick meeting with everybody.
KURT	Before the meeting …
MR. MEYER	What is it, Kurt?
KURT	We say: "Sadie stays!"

"What am I going to do?"

MRS. MEYER	Excuse me?
ANN	Sadie goes … then we go, too!
THE OFFICE WORKERS	Yes, that's right.
ALVIN	Sadie isn't slow.
MIA	She does a lot of work. She often works late.
LIZ	(*quickly*) She's a good team leader.

JIM	(*quickly*) She's smart.
DYLAN	(*quickly*) We want Sadie, not Joe!
SADIE:	Team! Stop! Mr. and Mrs. Meyer are trying to talk.
KURT	We don't want a new team leader.
MRS. MEYER	(*surprised*) A new team leader?
SADIE	They mean Joe.
MRS MEYER	Oh, yes, Joe. Sadie, you're going to meet Joe later. Maybe he can work on your team.
MR. MEYER	You need another worker, Sadie.
MRS. MEYER	Yes and *we* want to say thank you to the team.
MR. MEYER	We have a surprise.
MRS. MEYER	Everybody in this office needs a vacation. And everybody in this office needs a raise. Right?
THE OFFICE WORKERS	(*with big smiles*) Oh, yes, we do!
MRS MEYER	Everybody is going to have a raise and a vacation very soon.
THE OFFICE WORKERS	Yes!
MR. MEYER	Look, Gladys—Mrs. Meyer—happy workers with big smiles.
SADIE	This is a very big day at the office!
BEN	Yes, it *was* a very big day at the office.

ACTIVITIES

Pages 1–7

Before you read

1 Look at the Word List at the back of the book. What are the words in your language?

2 Look at the picture on page 2. Answer the questions.
   a What time is it?
   b How many offices are there in the picture?
   c How many people are there in the picture?

While you read

3 Write the names.
   a .... is a doorman.
   b .... are the bosses.
   c .... arrives after them.
   d Then .... arrives at work.
   e After her, ..., ..., and .... arrive.
   f .... walks into the office after them.
   g Then .... arrives, but he isn't late.
   h ...., the team leader, is late to work.

After you read

4 Everybody talks about today's surprise. What do they think? Find the right four words.

It's going to be a(n) ..... day.

bad   cold   difficult   happy   important   interesting
long   quiet

5 Write about the picture on page 6. What can you see? Who can you see? What are they doing? What are they thinking?

6 Work with another student. Ask and answer the questions.
   a Where do you work/go to school?
   b Do you like it? Why (not)?
   c Do you sometimes arrive late? Why? Is it a problem?

Pages 8–14

Before you read

7 Look at the picture on page 10.

    a Where are the people in this picture?

    b Why are they there?

While you read

8 Who is talking?

    a "Why is it a big day?"

    b "I'd like a raise."

    c "I need a vacation—soon."

    d "We can talk later."

    e "Quiet! I'm going to listen."

    f "We can talk about my idea."

    g "They're talking about you!"

    h "What am I going to do?"

After you read

9 Work with another student. Say the words. Then put them in the right places.

    Kate   moon   Mia   street   feet   Maria   June

    Korea   wait   soon

    a late, eight, ……..…..…, …..……..…..

    b meet, ……..…..…, …..……..…..

    c afternoon, ……..…..…, …..……..…, ……..…..…..

    d idea, ……..…..…, …..……..…, ……..…..…..

10 Are these sentences right or wrong?

    a Everybody is going to have a vacation.

    b The team needs a new worker.

    c Everybody is going to have a raise.

    d Sadie isn't going to be the team leader.

11 Write about a bad day at work or at school.